JAN 2020

SCIENCE **WHIZ**
EXPERIMENTS

EXPERIMENTS WITH THE HUMAN BODY

Robert Gardner

E **Enslow Publishing**
101 W. 23rd Street
Suite 240
New York, NY 10011
USA
enslow.com

Published in 2018 by Enslow Publishing, LLC.
101 W. 23rd Street, Suite 240, New York, NY 10011

Library of Congress Cataloging-in-Publication Data

Names: Gardner, Robert, 1929- author.
Title: Experiments with the human body / Robert Gardner.
Description: New York : Enslow Publishing, 2018. | Series: Science whiz
    experiments | Includes bibliographical references and index.
Identifiers: LCCN 2017001869 | ISBN 9780766086845 (library bound : alk. paper)
Subjects: LCSH: Human body—Experiments—Juvenile literature.
Classification: LCC QP37 .G3586 2018 | DDC 612—dc23
LC record available at https://lccn.loc.gov/2017001869

Printed in China

To Our Readers: We have done our best to make sure all website addresses in this book were active and appropriate when we went to press. However, the author and the publisher have no control over and assume no liability for the material available on those websites or on any websites they may link to. Any comments or suggestions can be sent by email to customerservice@enslow.com.

Illustrations by Joseph Hill

Photo Credits: Cover, p. 1, Sebastian Kaulitzki/Shutterstock.com; back cover and interior pages background pattern curiosity/Shutterstock.com.

Contents

Introduction

The human body is an incredible collection of cells. There are so many moving parts, both visible on the outside and microscopic on the inside. Your eyes see, your skin feels, and your digestive system turns food into energy. Your heart and lungs work together to get oxygen to your cells and get rid of carbon dioxide waste. The experiments in this book deal with the human body, from breathing and pumping blood to digesting food and sensing the world around you. It's a fun and fascinating way to learn how the human body works.

If you find that you enjoy learning about the human body by doing experiments, you may want to continue to do so by studying biology and related subjects in high school and college. It might even become part of your life's work if you become a doctor, nurse, medical technician, research scientist, or take up another occupation involving human biology.

At times, as you carry out the activities in this book, you may need a partner to help you. It would be best if you work with someone who enjoys experimenting as much as you do. In that way, you will both enjoy what you are doing. **If any danger is involved in doing an experiment, it will be made known to you. In some cases, to avoid danger, you will be asked to work with an adult. Please do so.** We don't want you to take any chances that could lead to an injury.

Like any good scientist, you will find it useful to record ideas, notes, data, and anything you can conclude from your investigations in a notebook. By doing so, you can keep track of the information you gather and the conclusions you reach. It will allow you to refer back to things you have done and help you in doing other projects in the future.

Entering a Science Fair

Some of the investigations in this book contain ideas you might use at a science fair. However, judges at science fairs do not reward projects or experiments that are simply copied from a book. For example, a diagram of the human eye would not impress most judges; however, a model of the human eye containing a lens that functions like the convex lens in the human eye would certainly attract their attention.

Science fair judges tend to reward creative thought and imagination. It is difficult to be creative or imaginative unless you are really interested in your project; therefore, try to choose an investigation that appeals to you. Before you jump into a project, consider, too, your own talents and the cost of the materials you will need.

If you decide to use an experiment or idea found in this book for a science fair, you should find ways to modify or extend it. This should not be difficult because you will discover that as you carry out investigations new ideas come to mind. Ideas will come to you that could make excellent science fair projects, particularly because the ideas are your own and are interesting to you.

If you decide to enter a science fair and have never done so, you should read some of the books listed in the Further Reading section. These books deal specifically with science fairs and will provide plenty of helpful hints and useful information that will help you to avoid the pitfalls that sometimes plague first-time entrants. You will learn how to prepare appealing reports that include charts and graphs, how to set up and display your work, how to present your project, and how to relate to judges and visitors.

Be Safe

Most of the projects included in this book are perfectly safe. However, the following safety rules are well worth reading before you start any project.

1. Never look directly at the sun! It can damage your eyes.

2. Do any experiments or projects, whether from this book or of your own design, **under the supervision of a science teacher or other knowledgeable adult**.

3. Read all instructions carefully before proceeding with a project. If you have questions, check with your supervisor before going any further.

4. Maintain a serious attitude while conducting experiments. Fooling around can be dangerous to you and to others.

5. Wear approved safety goggles when you are working with a flame or doing anything that might cause injury to your eyes.

6. Have a first aid kit nearby while you are experimenting.

7. Do not put your fingers or any object other than properly designed electrical connectors into electrical outlets.

8. Never let water droplets come in contact with a hot lightbulb.

9. Never experiment with household electricity.

10. The liquid in some thermometers is mercury (a dense liquid metal). It is dangerous to touch mercury or breathe mercury vapor, and such thermometers have been banned in many states. When doing these experiments, use only non-mercury thermometers, such as those filled with alcohol. If you have a mercury thermometer in the house, **ask an adult** if it can be taken to a local mercury thermometer exchange location.

Following the Scientific Method

Scientists look at the world and try to understand how things work. They make careful observations and conduct research. Different areas of science use different approaches. Depending on the problem, one method is likely to be better than another. Designing a new medicine for heart disease, studying the spread of an invasive plant such as purple loosestrife, and finding evidence of water on Mars all require different methods.

Despite the differences, all scientists use a similar general approach in doing experiments. This is called the scientific method. In most experiments, some or all of the following steps are used: observation of a problem, formulation of a question, making a hypothesis (an answer to the question), making a prediction (an if-then statement), designing and conducting an experiment, analysis of results, drawing conclusions, and accepting or rejecting the hypothesis. Scientists then share their findings by writing articles that are published.

You might wonder how to start an experiment. When you observe something, you may become curious and ask a question. Your question, which could arise from an earlier experiment or from reading, may be answered by a well-designed investigation. Once you have a question, you can make a hypothesis. Your hypothesis is a possible answer to the question. Once you have a hypothesis, it is time to design an experiment to test a consequence of your hypothesis.

In most cases you should do a controlled experiment. This means having two groups that are treated the same except for the one factor being tested. That factor is called a variable. For example, suppose your question is "Do green plants need light?" Your hypothesis might be that they do need light. To test the hypothesis, you would use two groups of green plants. One group is called the control group, the other is called the experimental group. The two groups should be treated the same except for one factor. Both should be planted in the same amount and type of soil, given the same amount of water, kept at the same temperature, and so forth. The control group would be placed in the dark. The experimental group would be put in the light. Light is the variable. It is the only difference between the two groups.

During the experiment, you would collect data. For example, you might measure the plants' growth in centimeters, count the number of living and dead leaves, and note the color and condition of the leaves. By comparing the data collected from the control and experimental groups over a few weeks, you would draw conclusions. Healthier growth and survival rates of plants grown in light would allow you to conclude that green plants need light.

Two other terms are often used in scientific experiments—dependent and independent variables. One dependent variable in this example is healthy growth, which depends on light being present. Light is the independent variable. It doesn't depend on anything.

After the data are collected, they are analyzed to see if it supports or rejects the hypothesis. The results of one experiment often lead you to a related question. Or they may send you off in a different direction. Whatever the results, something can be learned from every experiment.

Chapter 1

Circulation and Respiration

The circulatory system and respiratory system of the human body work together. The heart pumps blood throughout the body, bringing oxygen and taking away carbon dioxide. These gases are exchanged in the lungs. Deep inside your chest, your heart muscle contracts (beats) about once every second throughout your life. Each heartbeat pushes blood out of the heart's two ventricles into arteries that carry the blood to all parts of the body, including the lungs. After the heart contracts, it relaxes as blood from all over the body flows through veins into the heart's two atria.

The blood that flows out of the heart's right ventricle through the pulmonary artery travels to the lungs. (See Figures 1a and 1b.) There, oxygen in the air you have breathed (inspired) into your lungs diffuses into the blood. At the same time, waste gases in the blood diffuse into the air in the lungs. These gases are ejected from the body when you exhale (move air out of the lungs).

The oxygen-rich blood flows back into the heart's left atrium through the pulmonary veins. From there it moves to the left ventricle as the atria contract. Shortly thereafter, the ventricles contract and the oxygenated blood travels through the aorta to arterial branches that carry the blood to all parts of the body. After the blood transfers oxygen to the cells of the body, it returns to the heart through veins leading to the superior and inferior vena cava. These large veins carry the blood to the right atrium. From there it is pushed into the right ventricle as the atria contract. The blood has made a complete circuit. It will again be pushed into the pulmonary artery as the ventricles contract. This circulation of blood is shown in Figure 1a.

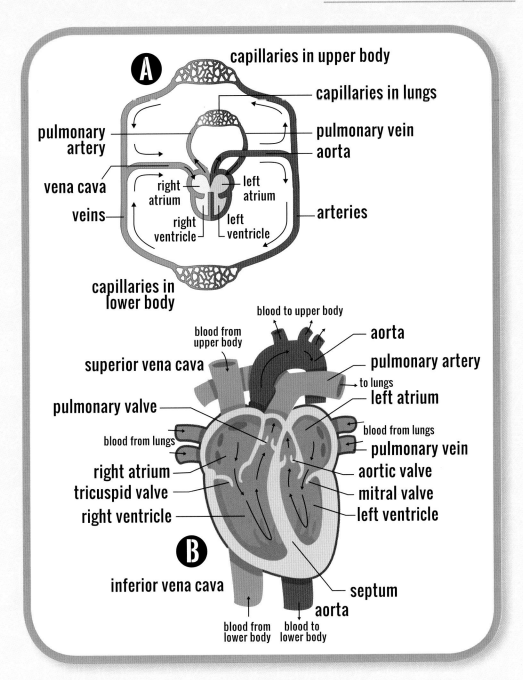

Figure 1. A) A general picture shows the human circulatory system. B) A more detailed drawing shows the heart and the major arteries and veins leading from and to it. Notice that arteries carry blood away from the heart and veins carry blood to the heart.

1.1 Pulse Rate

> **THINGS YOU WILL NEED:**
> - clay
> - drinking straw
> - a partner

When your heart beats (contracts), it pushes blood into your main arteries. Arteries are elastic. Like a rubber band, they stretch when more blood is pumped into them. They contract between heartbeats. Arterial expansion can be felt in arteries that are close to the surface of your body. What you feel is called a pulse because the arteries pulsate (throb) when the heart beats.

1. You have probably had a nurse take your pulse, but you can take your own. Put your first two fingers on the inside of your wrist just below the point where your thumb connects with your wrist (see Figure 2).

   Your pulse rate is the number of pulses you feel per minute, but you don't have to count for a full minute. Counting the number of pulses over a 15-second period and multiplying by four will give you your heart rate in beats per minute.

2. To amplify your pulse to make its effect visible, place your hand, palm upward, on a table. Put a small lump of clay on your pulse point. Stick a straw upright in the clay. What happens to the straw each time your heart beats?

3. Arteries are close to the surface at other points in your body. You can find another pulse on either side of your larynx (Adam's apple). Can you find a pulse just in front of your ear? Can you find a pulse on the inside of your elbow? How about your ankle?

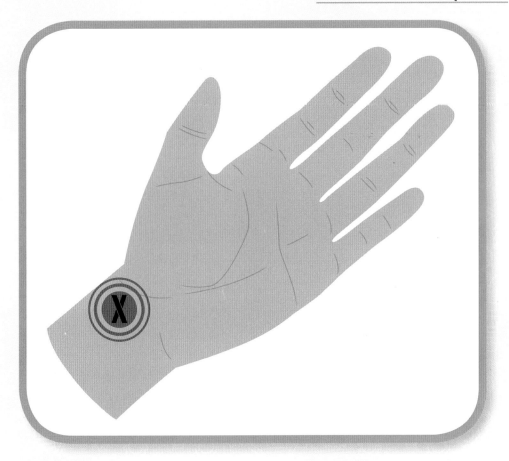

Figure 2. The X shows you where to place your fingers on a left wrist in order to feel a pulse.

4. Take a partner's pulse at his neck and his wrist at the same time. Which pulse do you expect to feel first? Try it! Were you right?

   Your heart, which is about the size of a fist, only weighs about 290 grams (10.2 ounces). But it is a mighty and amazing pump. Each time your heart beats, it pushes about 130 mL (4.6 oz) of blood into your arteries.

5. Assuming your heart beats about 70 times each minute, how many milliliters of blood does it pump in one minute?

6. A liter (L) is 1,000 ml. How many liters of blood does your heart pump each minute?

7. A liter is equal to 1.06 quarts. How many quarts of blood does your heart pump every minute? How many gallons per minute?

8. How many liters of blood does your heart pump each hour? Each day? (See the Answers section at the back of the book.) Do you agree that your heart is a mighty and amazing pump?

Using an anatomy book, identify the major arteries and veins of the human body. After studying these vessels, where might you expect to find pulses? Can you find them?

1.2 The Sound of Your Heart

THINGS YOU WILL NEED:
- stethoscope or a partner
- clock with a second hand

If you have access to a stethoscope, you can listen to your own heart.

1. Place the ear tips in your ears and the chest piece slightly to the left of the center of your chest. Move the chest piece slightly until you hear the heart sounds clearly. Listen for two sounds in close succession. The first is a relatively long booming sound. The second is a short, sharp sound. Together they sound like "lubb-dup." The "lubb" is caused by the contracting heart muscle and the closing of the valves between the atria and ventricles. The "dup" is the sound of the aortic and pulmonary valves slamming shut as the heart relaxes. At that time, the heart is no longer pushing the blood so the blood tries to reenter the heart. However, the valves that connect the ventricles to the aorta and pulmonary arteries are like a door to a room. They open only one way (out, into the arteries). When the blood tries to flow back to the heart, the valves close with a loud "dup" sound.

2. If you don't have a stethoscope, you can hear the same sounds by placing your ear against the chest of a partner. Your partner will probably want to hear your heart as well.

3. While listening to a heart, count the number of times it beats in one minute. Does it agree with the count you measure by taking your pulse? The number of times your heart beats in one minute is your heart rate. It is the number of beats per minute. What is your heart rate?

4. Which should happen first, hearing the heart beat or feeling a pulse? Do an experiment to test your prediction.

1.3 Veins and Valves

After blood pumped from the heart passes through the arteries and capillaries, it begins its journey back to the heart. The vessels that carry blood to the heart are called veins. The pressure in these vessels is much less than it is in the arteries. In fact, without the body's muscles squeezing the veins, blood would collect in the veins of the lower body. Muscles are aided by the veins' one-way valves. These valves allow blood to move only one way—toward the heart.

1. Many veins are near your body's surface. You can see them through your skin. They have a bluish tint. In fact, they sometimes bulge along the skin on the back of your hand or on the inside of your forearm. If you have difficulty seeing a vein, let your arm hang down for a few seconds. Blood will collect in these veins.

2. Once you can see your veins clearly, put your thumb on one of the veins in your forearm or the back of your hand. Then "sweep" the blood in the vein toward your heart by moving the index finger of the same hand along the vein. Gradually increase the distance you move your finger. When you reach a valve, the vein below the valve will collapse and become difficult to see when you lift your finger. You will see the blood-filled vein above the valve but not below it. When you release your thumb, blood will flow through the vein again. Can you locate the next valve along the vein?

3. Let your hand hang by your side for a few seconds. When you can clearly see the veins on the back of one hand, slowly

raise that hand. What happens when your hand is well above your heart? Can you explain why?

4. Hold one hand over your head for 20 seconds. Let the other one hang at your side. Then look at the back of both hands. One hand has more color than the other. Which one is it? Why do you think one hand has more color than the other?

What is an electrocardiogram? Examine an electrocardiogram. What is the significance of each part of the pattern? How does a cardiologist use an electrocardiogram to look for defects in a patient's heart?

1.4 Breathing Mechanics

There are two actions that go on as long as you live: your heart beats and you breathe. Normally, you are not aware of either.

1. To get a feel for what happens when you breathe, lie on your back. Place one hand on your stomach. What do you feel when you inhale (breathe in)? When you exhale?

2. Take a deep breath. Are the feelings the same, only more so?

3. Sit up. Put your hands on the sides of your chest. What do you feel when you take a deep breath? Can you explain what is happening?

You felt your stomach rise when you inhaled. You felt it fall when you exhaled. When you inhale, you can feel your chest rise and expand. As air leaves your lungs, you feel your chest fall and become smaller.

The muscles that control breathing are the diaphragm and the muscles between the ribs. The diaphragm (Figure 3a) is a large flat muscle that separates the thorax (chest) from the abdomen. When it contracts, it makes the chest cavity (the space inside the chest that is filled with the lungs) bigger. It also pushes down on the abdomen forcing it outward, which is what you felt. Contraction of rib muscles (Figure 3b) lifts the ribs upward and outward. This action enlarges the chest. As these muscles and the diaphragm relax, the diaphragm moves up and the chest moves downward and inward causing the chest cavity to shrink.

But what causes air to move into and out of the lungs? This is best understood by making a model of the chest, lungs, and diaphragm.

4. To do this, **ask an adult** to cut off the lower half of an empty 2-liter, clear, plastic soda bottle. The bottle's upper half represents your chest cavity.

5. Find an old balloon that has been inflated several times but does not leak. Slip the neck of the balloon over the mouth of the bottle. Let the rest of the balloon hang inside the bottle as shown in Figure 3c. The balloon represents one of your lungs.

6. Stretch clear plastic wrap over the open bottom of the bottle. Hold the plastic in its stretched condition with one or more rubber bands around the bottle. The plastic wrap represents your diaphragm.

7. Attach half of a strip of clear plastic tape to the center of the plastic wrap. Hold the other half between two fingers. Use your other hand to hold the bottle. Use the strip of plastic tape to pull the "diaphragm" downward.

Watch what happens to the balloon when you pull the "diaphragm" downward. What happens when the "diaphragm" moves back up? How does this model help explain the process of breathing? (See the Answers section at the back of the book for an answer.)

8. When you have a cold, your nose is often filled with mucus. Fortunately, you are still able to breathe. Hold your nose. Can you still breathe? How does the air reach your lungs? Now close your mouth and release your nose. How does the air reach your lungs? What must be true about your mouth and nose?

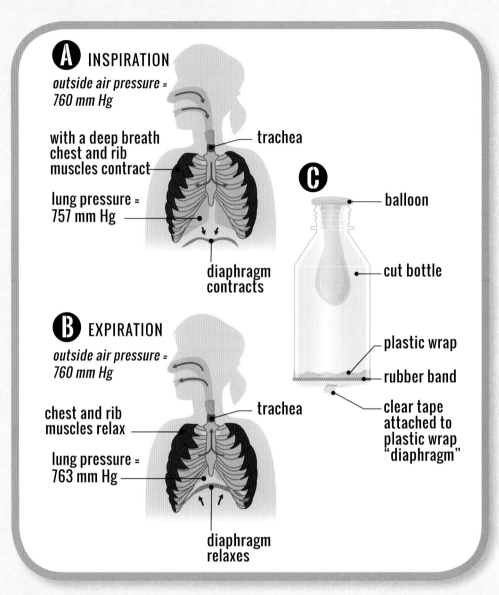

A INSPIRATION

*outside air pressure =
760 mm Hg*

with a deep breath
chest and rib
muscles contract

lung pressure =
757 mm Hg

trachea

diaphragm
contracts

C

balloon

cut bottle

plastic wrap

rubber band

clear tape
attached to
plastic wrap
"diaphragm"

B EXPIRATION

*outside air pressure =
760 mm Hg*

chest and rib
muscles relax

lung pressure =
763 mm Hg

trachea

diaphragm
relaxes

Figure 3. A) and B) Air enters the lungs during inspiration. Inspiration occurs when the diaphragm and rib muscles contract. These contractions increase the size (volume) of the thoracic cavity (chest). The increased volume lowers the pressure in the lungs below that of the air outside the body. As a result, air rushes into the lungs. During expiration, those muscles relax. The diaphragm moves upward, the ribs fall, and the volume of the chest cavity shrinks. This causes the pressure of air inside the lungs to become greater than the air pressure outside the body. As a result, air is pushed out of the lungs. C) A model explains how we breathe.

Place a cloth measuring tape around a friend's chest at armpit level. What happens to the circumference of his chest when he takes a deep breath? What happens to the circumference of his chest when he expires as much air as possible? Now place the tape measure around his abdomen at belly button (navel) level. What happens to the circumference of his abdomen when he takes a deep breath? What happens to it after he expires as much air as possible? Design a means of measuring the front-to-back thickness of your friend's chest and abdomen following a deep inhalation and a forceful expiration.

Build a better model of breathing that includes two lungs and both a diaphragm and the ribs that move up and out during inspiration.

What happens to the lungs when the chest cavity is opened during open heart surgery?

What keeps the lungs from collapsing completely when someone exhales?

1.5 Find the Breathing Rate

THINGS YOU WILL NEED:

- a partner
- couch or floor with soft carpet
- watch or clock with a second hand
- notebook
- pen or pencil

Your heart rate is the number of times your heart beats per minute. Your breathing rate is the number of times you inhale or exhale in one minute.

1. Have a partner lie down on his or her back. Watch your partner's chest or abdomen rise and fall. How can you tell when he or she is inhaling or exhaling? Using a watch or clock with a second hand, determine your partner's breathing rate.

2. Have your partner determine your breathing rate while you lie on your back. What is your breathing rate? How does it compare to your partner's breathing rate?

What causes hiccups? How are they related to breathing? There are lots of "cures" for hiccups. Do any of them work?

1.6 Exhaling Carbon Dioxide

THINGS YOU WILL NEED:

- **an adult**
- clay
- birthday candle
- matches
- empty one-quart glass jar
- clock or watch with a second hand
- notebook
- pen or pencil
- water
- cardboard
- scissors
- dishpan
- plastic tubing or flexible drinking straw

Matches and breathing into a paper bag are involved in this experiment. It needs to be done **under close adult supervision**.

You have probably heard that you inhale oxygen and exhale carbon dioxide. And you may know that oxygen makes up only 21 percent of the air. Consequently, you don't inhale pure oxygen. Do you exhale pure carbon dioxide?

To test the carbon dioxide (CO_2) content of exhaled air, you can compare the time that a candle will burn in a volume of air and in the same volume of lung air (air from your lungs). If lung air is pure carbon dioxide, the candle should go out immediately because carbon dioxide does not support combustion. That is why CO_2 is used in some fire extinguishers.

1. To carry out this experiment, use a small piece of clay to support a birthday candle. **Under adult supervision**, light the candle. Let it burn for about 15 seconds. Then invert an empty one-quart glass jar and put it over the candle as shown in Figure 4a. Use a clock or a watch that can measure seconds to find out how long the candle will burn in the air-filled jar. Record that time in your notebook.

2. Next, remove the jar and, **under adult supervision**, relight the candle. Fill the jar with water, cover its mouth with a square piece of cardboard, and invert it in a pan of water (Figure 4b).

3. Take a deep breath. Then fill the inverted jar by expelling your lung air through a piece of plastic tubing into the jar. Your bubbles of lung air will replace the water in the jar (Figure 4c). Remove the jar from the water. Quickly place it over the burning candle. How long does the candle burn in lung air? Record the result.

4. Repeat the experiment, but this time hold the air in your lungs for about 20 seconds before you use it to fill the jar. How long will the candle burn in lung air that has been in your lungs for about 20 seconds? Is the candle's burn time different than when you filled the balloon with lung air immediately after it had been inhaled? If it is, can you explain why?

Effect of Rebreathing Air

What will happen to your breathing rate and depth of breathing if you repeatedly breathe the same air? To find out, you will need a paper bag. Do not use a plastic bag.

5. **Under adult supervision,** place the opening of the paper bag tightly around your nose and mouth so that no fresh air can reach your lungs. Breathe and rebreathe the air in the bag for a minute or two. What happens to your breathing rate? What happens to your depth of breathing (the volume of air you take into your lungs with each breath)? How can you explain the changes that occur?

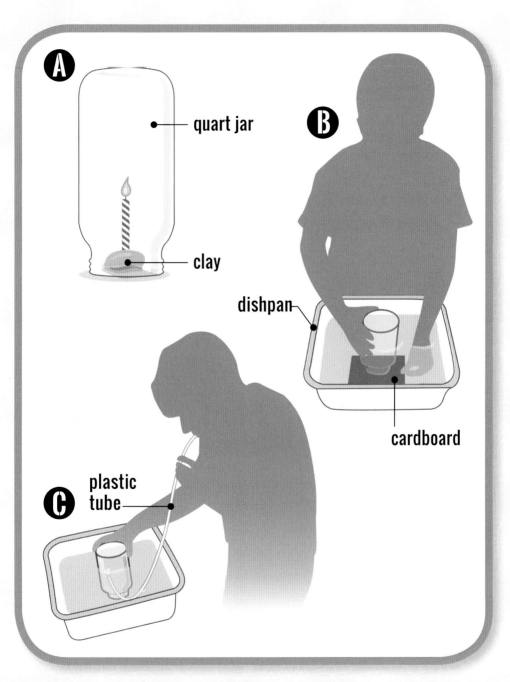

Figure 4. Is exhaled air pure carbon dioxide?

Ordinary air is about 21 percent oxygen and 0.04 percent carbon dioxide. The concentration of nitrogen in both inhaled and exhaled air is 78 percent. Design and carry out an experiment to determine the percentage of oxygen and carbon dioxide in exhaled air.

Measuring Blood Pressure

THINGS YOU WILL NEED:

- **an adult**
- battery-operated blood pressure monitor or sphygmomanometer
- a partner
- couch or floor with soft carpet
- notebook

When you inflate a balloon, you force air into the balloon. The pressure of the air inside the balloon increases. When your heart contracts, it pushes more blood into your arteries. This causes the arteries to expand and the pressure of the blood pushing against the arterial walls increases.

When someone measures blood pressure, they measure both systolic and diastolic pressures. Systolic pressure occurs when the heart contracts, forcing blood into the arteries. Diastolic pressure occurs just before the heart contracts, when the pressure in the arteries is at a minimum.

When blood pressure is recorded, the higher systolic pressure is recorded first, followed by the diastolic pressure. A normal record of blood pressure might read 120/70, measured in millimeters (mm) of mercury. The pressure of the earth's atmosphere at sea level, which we measure with a barometer, is normally 760 mm of mercury. This means that the air can support a column of mercury 760 mm high. This is the same pressure as 10.1 newtons per square centimeter or 14.7 pounds per square inch. Of course, blood, like the rest of your body, is subject to air pressure. Consequently, blood pressure is the pressure by which the blood exceeds the pressure of the air.

Knowing the systolic and diastolic blood pressure, you can easily calculate what is known as pulse pressure. It is the difference between systolic and diastolic blood pressure. In the example given above, the pulse pressure would be

120 – 70 = 50 mm of mercury.

The easiest way to measure blood pressure is with a battery-operated monitor that fits over a person's index finger or wrist. It gives a digital display of both systolic and diastolic pressure. Still another battery-powered blood pressure monitor inflates at the press of a button. It gives a digital display of blood pressure and pulse rate. Your family may have such an instrument or you may be able to borrow one.

The traditional device for measuring blood pressure is the sphygmomanometer [SFIG moh muh NAH mih tur] found in doctors' offices. It is more difficult to operate than the automatic devices. It consists of a cuff that is placed around a person's upper arm and then inflated. When the pressure in the cuff exceeds the pressure of the blood flowing through the brachial artery in the upper arm, the artery collapses and blood flow stops. By slowly reducing the pressure in the cuff, a point is reached at which systolic pressure allows a spurt of blood to pass through the artery. The short spurt of blood produces a sound that can be heard by placing a stethoscope over the artery on the inside of the elbow. When the first sound is heard, the pressure is read on a gauge—or manometer—attached to the cuff.

As the pressure in the cuff is reduced further, the sound becomes more muffled. The sound eventually disappears when the cuff no longer restricts any blood flow. Consequently, the sound's disappearance indicates the subject's diastolic or minimum blood pressure.

1. Use one of the automatic blood pressure devices. If you have to use a sphygmomanometer, **ask an adult** familiar with taking blood pressures to help you. Be sure that the cuff does not restrict a subject's blood flow for more than a few seconds.

    Ask a partner (**if you use a sphygmomanometer, your partner should be an adult**) to help you with this experiment. Lie on your back on a couch or a floor with a soft carpet. Rest quietly for five minutes. After that time, your partner will determine your blood pressure. Record the pressure in a notebook. What was your blood pressure while lying down? What was your pulse pressure?

2. Stand up. Your partner will again determine your blood pressure and pulse pressure. Record the data. What was your blood pressure and pulse pressure after you stood?

What might you do to increase your blood pressure?

What might you do to reduce your blood pressure?

1.8 Exercise Effects

THINGS YOU WILL NEED:

- 3 partners
- 2 watches or clocks with second hands
- device to measure blood pressure
- notebook
- pen or pencil
- graph paper

To do this experiment you will need three partners. One will measure breathing rates, another will measure pulse rates, and the third will serve as a subject. You will measure blood pressures. (If you can't find three partners, you can do the experiment in three parts with just one partner.)

1. Have one partner serve as the subject. Have him lie on his back on a couch or soft rug and rest quietly for five minutes. Then have a partner measure the subject's breathing rate. Have a second partner measure the subject's pulse rate on the wrist of one arm while you take the subject's blood pressure on the other arm. Record all the results in a notebook.

2. Have the subject sit upright. After five minutes, you and your partners will determine and record the subject's breathing rate, pulse rate, and blood pressure.

3. Ask the subject to stand up. After five minutes, you and your partners will determine and record the subject's breathing rate, pulse rate, and blood pressure.

4. Finally, have the subject run in place for five minutes. As soon as he stops running, you and your partners will determine and record the subject's breathing rate, pulse rate, and blood pressure. Continue to make these measurements at

two-minute intervals until pulse rate, breathing rate, and blood pressure return to, or very nearly to, the rates and pressure he had before exercising.

5. Plot a graph (in minutes) of the subject's breathing rate, pulse rate, and blood pressure versus time for the period following the exercise. It can all be done on one graph similar to the one in Figure 5. What can you conclude from the graph?

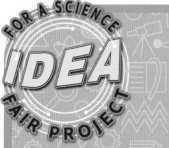

Measure the breathing and heart rates and blood pressures of a number of different people after they have been lying, sitting, standing, and exercising. Does a subject's age or sex seem to affect the results? Do you notice differences in your data for people who are in good physical shape, such as athletes, and for people who are not "in shape"? If you do, what are those differences and how can you account for them?

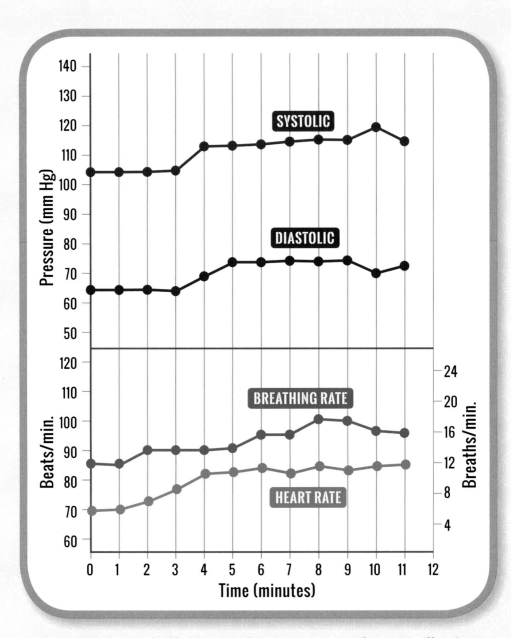

Figure 5. Draw graphs like these to show how position and exercise affect heart rate, breathing rate, and blood pressure.

Chapter 2

Sensing Your World

The human body has five senses. Ears are for hearing, eyes are for seeing, and the tongue is for tasting. You smell with your nose and feel with your skin. There is so much science involved with your senses.

To see, light must reach your eyes. You hear when sound waves reach your ears. The study of light and sound waves is part of physics.

You smell when molecules of scented substances reach your nose. You taste with your tongue, but, as you will discover, what we commonly call taste is actually a combination of taste and smell.

Touch, which includes sensitivity to pressure, pain, and temperature, is a sense that is spread over most of your skin. People can survive without sight, hearing, smell, or taste, but touch is essential to life.

2.1 Hearing Sound

Your ears are your access to the world of sound. Sounds are caused by vibrations that create pulses of air pressure. These pulses travel to your ear where they cause your eardrum (see Figure 6) to vibrate.

The vibrations are carried across your middle ear by three small bones. The third bone, the stirrup, vibrates against the oval window of the inner ear. This causes the cochlear fluid in the snail-shaped inner ear (cochlea) to vibrate. The basilar membrane lies within the cochlear fluid. This membrane varies in width and thickness. High frequency sounds, like those from a soprano's voice, cause the narrow part of the membrane to vibrate. Low frequency sounds, like those from an electric bass guitar, cause the wider parts of the membrane to vibrate. Tiny fibers (hair cells) connected to the basilar membrane are stimulated by the vibrating membrane. Nerve cells at the base of the hair cells respond to basilar vibrations and send impulses to the brain along the auditory nerve. It is in the brain that we actually hear sounds.

To see how your inner ear responds to sounds of different frequency, you can do several experiments. All objects that vibrate, such as the strings of a piano or the basilar membrane in your inner ear, have natural frequencies. For example, the A key above middle C on a piano strikes a string that vibrates at 440 Hz. (Hz is the symbol for frequency. One vibration per second is 1 Hz.) If you sing a note that has a frequency of 440 Hz, a piano string will resonate (respond

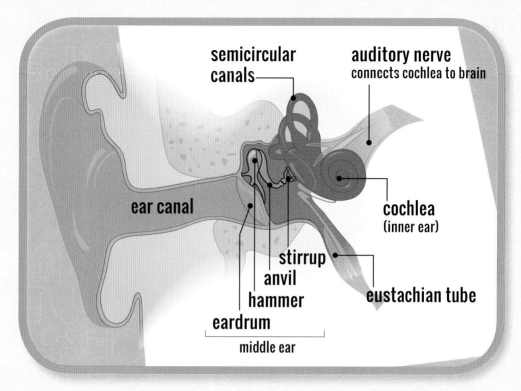

Figure 6. A diagram shows the many parts of the human ear.

by vibrating at its natural frequency of 440 Hz). The vibrational response of any object to its natural frequency is called resonance.

1. Open a piano. Use your foot to hold down the pedal on the right (the sustaining pedal). This lifts the dampers so that the strings can vibrate freely. Sing a note loudly and clearly. Then listen carefully. You will hear sounds coming from the strings that resonate to the note you sang.

2. Resonance can also be produced in air columns such as those found in a pipe organ. To see this effect, put your lower lip against the edge of the mouth of an empty 1-liter plastic soda bottle. Blow across the mouth of the bottle. You should hear a low pitched sound caused by air vibrating in the bottle.

3. Hold the same bottle next to your ear. Have a partner blow across an identical bottle. What do you hear coming from your bottle? What does your partner hear when you blow into your bottle?

4. Repeat the experiment, but this time have your partner blow into a 2-liter plastic bottle while you listen with a 1-liter bottle. What is different this time? How do the sounds made with the 1-liter and 2-liter bottles differ?

5. You might have heard that you can hear the sea by holding a conch shell against your ear. You can hear the same effect by holding an empty mailing tube open at both ends against your ear. The air column in the tube will resonate to any sounds that match the air column's natural frequency of vibration. Hold mailing tubes of different lengths against your ear. You will find that the pitch of the sound differs. The longer the tube, the lower the pitch of the sound you hear.

In your inner ear, it is the basilar membrane in the cochlea that resonates to the vibrations of the fluid in the cochlea.

IDEAS FOR A SCIENCE FAIR PROJECT

Carry out an investigation to find out why the pitch of the resonant sound heard in a mailing tube increases when you move the tube a short distance from your ear.

What is the eustachian tube (see Figure 6) and what function does it serve?

2.2 **Locating Sounds**

THINGS YOU WILL NEED:

- a piece of wide-diameter tubing about 1 meter (3 feet) long (a vacuum cleaner hose works well, but garden hose or plastic tubing about an inch in diameter will be satisfactory)
- tape
- a partner
- a pencil

Some animals can turn their ears toward the source of a sound. Our ears don't move very much, but we can usually tell the direction from which a sound is coming. To see how we do this, you can do an experiment.

1. Find a piece of wide-diameter tubing about 1 meter (3 feet) long. A vacuum cleaner hose works well, but you can use a length of old garden hose or plastic tubing about an inch in diameter. Stick a piece of tape to the exact middle of the tube.

2. Hold the tubing in front of you. Place the ends of the tubing against opposite ears. Have a partner support the center of the tubing with a finger. Close your eyes. Ask your partner to lightly tap the tube at different places with a pencil. Can you tell whether the sound is coming from the left or right side of the tube? If you can, ask your partner to tap the middle of the tube. Can you tell that the sound is coming from a point directly in front of you?

3. Ask your partner to tap the tube at points close to the middle point. How far from the middle must the sound come before you can tell that it is to the right or left of the center?

4. Repeat this experiment with the tube behind you. Are the results the same?

5. Repeat the experiment, but listen with only one ear. Put cotton in your other ear. Can you locate the direction of sound sources with one ear?

As you may have guessed, we detect the location of sounds by the difference in time that it takes the sound to reach each ear. Sounds to your right reach your right ear before they reach your left ear and vice versa.

Do you think someone who is deaf in one ear finds it difficult to locate the source of sounds?

Sound normally travels at a speed of 330 meters per second (m/s). Use this information to determine the minimum time difference required in order to determine that a sound is to your right or left. Is this minimum time the same for everyone?

2.3 Keeping Your Balance

THINGS YOU WILL NEED:
- **an adult**
- **wide drinking glass**
- water
- food coloring

Look again at Figure 6. Notice the three semi-circular canals connected to the cochlea. They are part of the inner ear. These canals contain a fluid. When you move, the fluid shifts and pushes against tiny hairlike sensors. If you start to lose your balance, the sensors "tell" the brain to send messages to muscles that restore your balance.

1. Sometimes the sensory nerves in your semicircular canals can be fooled. To see how this might happen, **ask an adult** to stand near you in case you start to fall after, or while, doing this experiment. Turn around quickly in one place five or six times. Then stop. You will feel dizzy and may have trouble keeping your balance.

2. To see why your semicircular canals were fooled, try this. Add water to a wide drinking glass until it is about one-third full. Place a food coloring dispenser beside the glass. Swirl the glass. The water, like the fluid in your semicircular canals when you spin, will swirl. Then put the glass down and immediately add a drop of food coloring to the water. Does the water continue to swirl after you put the glass down? Do you think the fluid in your semicircular canals will continue to move after you stop spinning around?

   If it does, what message is it sending to your brain?

Does vision play a role in maintaining balance? Do an experiment to find out.

2.4 Tongue and Taste

1. Using a cotton swab, dab a little blue food coloring on the tip of your tongue. Then stick out your tongue in front of a magnifying mirror. The tiny round papillae (Figure 7a) where your taste buds (the cells sensitive to taste) are found will be a lighter color than the rest of your tongue. Do you have a lot of papillae?

   People with lots of papillae (about one-fourth of the population) are known as "supertasters." Supertasters may find vegetables bitter and are often skinny because they are picky eaters.

   Each taste bud responds primarily to one taste. Taste buds sensitive to each kind of taste are clustered on different parts of the tongue. You can do an experiment to find out which parts of the tongue respond to a particular taste.

2. Prepare the following solutions: a) 10 grams of kosher salt in 100 mL of water (a salty-tasting substance); b) 10 grams of sugar in 100 mL of water (a sweet-tasting substance); c) 20 mL of clear vinegar in 80 mL of water (a sour-tasting

substance). You will also need a few milliliters of tonic water, which contains bitter-tasting quinine.

3. In your notebook, make four drawings of a tongue like the one shown in Figure 7b. Label the drawings "salt," "sweet," "sour," and "bitter."

4. Ask a partner to stick out her tongue. Dip a cotton swab into the salt solution. Apply the wet swab (Figure 7c) to the tip of your partner's tongue (the region marked "1" in your drawing). If your partner senses the salty taste, mark that region of your drawing with a plus (+) sign (Figure 7d). If she senses no taste, mark the region with a minus (–) sign. Repeat the experiment for the sides of the tongue (regions 2 and 3), the center of the tongue (region 4), and the back of the tongue (region 5).

5. Have your partner rinse her mouth with water. Using a new swab, repeat the experiment to test for a sweet taste.

6. Rinse again, use a new swab, and repeat the experiment for a sour taste.

7. Repeat Step 6 for a bitter taste, using a new swab.

8. Now have your partner map your tongue to find which regions are sensitive to each taste.

9. Compare the results of the two experiments—the one on your partner and the one on you. Don't be surprised if they differ. People differ in the way their taste buds are spread across their tongues.

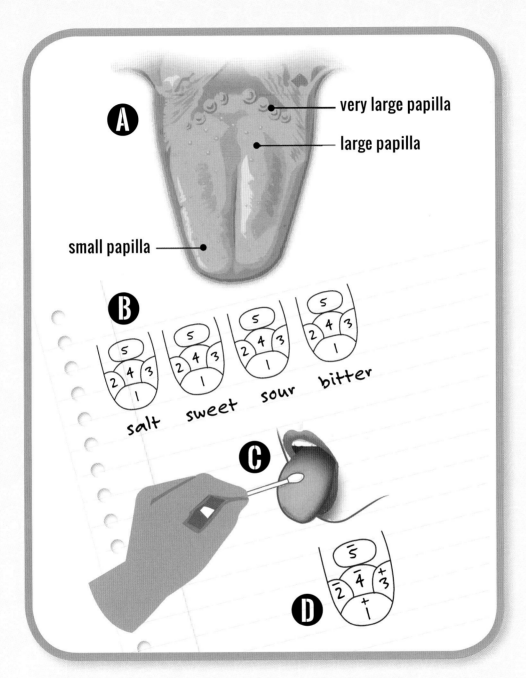

Figure 7. A) There are papillae on the tongue. B) Make four drawings showing regions of the tongue. C) Use a cotton swab to apply solutions to the different regions of the tongue. D) Record your results for each solution using plus (+) and minus (−) signs as shown.

2.5 Smell and Taste

Have you ever noticed how "blah" even your favorite foods taste when you have a cold? In this experiment you will find out why this happens.

1. Obtain the following liquids: milk, orange juice, pickle juice, and onion juice. Place the liquids in small paper or plastic cups.

2. Ask a partner to join you. Blindfold your partner. Ask your partner to hold her nose. Then ask your partner to taste each liquid in turn. She should rinse her mouth with water between tastings. Can your partner identify the taste? Can she identify the liquids being tasted? Record your results in a chart like the one below.

Liquid	Nose Closed		Nose Open	
	Taste	Identified as	Taste	Identified as

3. Repeat the experiment. This time reverse the order in which the liquids are tasted and do not have her hold her nose. This will allow the sense of smell as well as taste to be in effect.

Based on your results, do you think the sense of smell is involved in the way foods taste? Why do you think your food tastes "blah" when you have a cold?

Do people tend to lose their sense of taste as they grow older? Do an experiment to find out.

2.6 **Sense of Touch**

> **THINGS YOU WILL NEED:**
>
> - a partner
> - tennis ball
> - baseball
> - an orange
> - an apple
> - a peach

1. Blindfold a partner. Then ask your partner to try to identify some different spherical objects by touching them first with an elbow, then with a bare foot, and finally with fingers. The objects you provide might include a tennis ball, a baseball, an orange, an apple, and a peach.

2. After the person has tried to identify the spheres, you might let him or her confirm the guess by using his or her sense of smell.

Based on the results of this experiment, do you think the skin on the elbow, the foot, or the fingers has the greatest number of cells sensitive to touch? To confirm your prediction you can do another experiment.

2.7 Cells and Touch

1. Make a simple "touch tester." Stick two straight pins into a flat eraser or a piece of Styrofoam (see Figure 8). The pins should be about half a centimeter (0.5 cm or 5 mm) apart. Ask your partner to close his or her eyes.

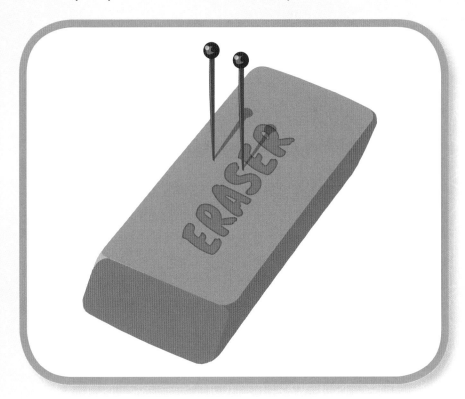

Figure 8. You can make a simple "touch tester."

2. Touch the pins very gently to the tip of your partner's index finger. Ask your partner, "Do you feel anything?" If the response is, "Yes," then ask, "Do you feel one or two points?"

3. Repeat the experiment on your partner's other fingers and thumb. Then experiment on his or her toes and elbow. You might also test your partner's palm, back of the hand, different parts of the arm, lips, ears, neck, and back. **Do not put the pins near anyone's eyes or inside their ears.**

4. Repeat the experiment, but this time set the pins about one centimeter apart. On which parts of the body are touch receptors most abundant? On which parts of the body are touch receptors least abundant? How do you know?

5. Ask your partner to close his or her eyes. Use a pencil tip to move single hairs on your partner's arm. Can your partner detect the touch? Are there touch receptors at the base of hairs? Do all hairs respond to touch? How about hairs on the head or the back of the neck?

Chapter 3

Eyes to See

When you think of vision, you probably think of your eyes. After all, it is the main way that humans sense the things around them. That is why an entire chapter is devoted to the eye and the sense of sight. However, you actually "see" not in your eyes but in your brain. The sensory cells that respond to light are located in your retinas, the layers of cells that line the rear interior surface of your eyeballs (see Figure 9). When light strikes these retinal cells, the cells send impulses along the optic nerve that leads to the visual center at the back of your brain. It is there that the images formed on the retina are interpreted and seen.

The human eye is a marvelous organ. It is shaped like a ball, hence the term "eyeball." It consists of three main layers.

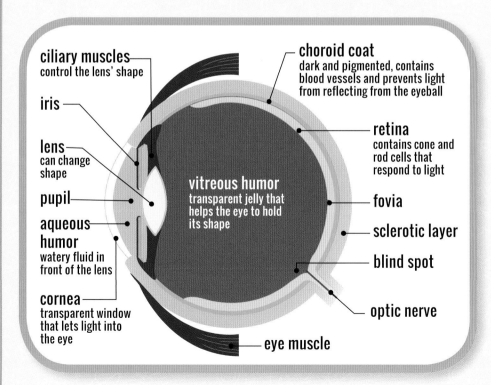

Figure 9. A cross-section drawing shows parts of the human eye.

The sclerotic coat, the outside layer, is white and sufficiently rigid to give the eye its spherical shape. Inside the sclerotic coat, the black choroid layer contains blood vessels. Its dark color reduces the reflection of light that enters the eye. The inner layer, the retina, contains the rod and cone cells that respond to light and send nerve impulses to the brain. The center of the retina, known as the fovea, has an abundance of cone cells and is the region where our best vision is located.

At the front of our eyes, the sclerotic coat becomes clear, forming the cornea. The cornea bends (refracts) light before it to passes through the pupil, an opening in the colored iris. The lens refracts the light further, causing images to form on the retina. The lens can be made more or less convex by the ciliary muscles. As a result, images of both near and distant objects can be focused on the retina. The aqueous and vitreous humors are fluids that fill the eyeball and maintain its spherical shape. Six muscles connected to each eyeball allow us to move our eyes up, down, sideways, and obliquely.

3.1 The Retina and Images

THINGS YOU WILL NEED:

- convex lens (a magnifying glass is a convex lens)
- a wall opposite a window

In order for you to see, your eye forms images on your retina. The cornea and lens at the front of your eye create the images from the light that passes through them. To see how this works, you can do an experiment.

1. Hold a convex lens (a magnifying glass is a convex lens) next to a wall that is opposite a window.

2. Move the lens closer to and farther from the wall until you see a clear image of outside objects on the wall. Notice that the images are upside down! But you don't see an upside down world unless you stand on your head. Somehow, you learned early in your life to deal with these inverted images. You see the world right side up.

   As an interesting experiment, several people have worn prisms in front of their eyes that created images on the retina that were right side up. For a while, they saw an upside down world. But within a few days they learned to see the world the way it really is. What do you think happened when they took off the prisms that caused the images on their retinas to be right side up?

3.2 The Human Eye

THINGS YOU WILL NEED:

- spherical or nearly spherical glass bowl, vase, or brandy glass
- black construction paper
- 60-watt frosted light bulb in a lamp socket
- sheet of cardboard
- sheet of white cardboard
- magnifying glass
- colored cellophane
- scissors
- room you can darken
- a partner
- water
- ruler
- transparent tape

1. Fill the spherical vessel with water. It represents the eyeball and the fluid inside the eyeball.

2. Cut an arrow about 2 cm long and 1/2 cm wide from colored cellophane. Use clear tape to center it inside a slightly larger square opening cut in a sheet of cardboard (see Figure 10a). The arrow represents an object whose image will be formed on the model's "retina." Make a hole about 0.5 cm (1/4 in) in diameter in the black construction paper. The hole represents the "pupil." Arrange the parts of your model as shown in Figure 10b. Notice that the object and "pupil" should be about as high as the center of the glass sphere.

3. Darken the room. Ask a partner to hold the light bulb so it is in line with the object, the "pupil," and the center of the "eyeball."

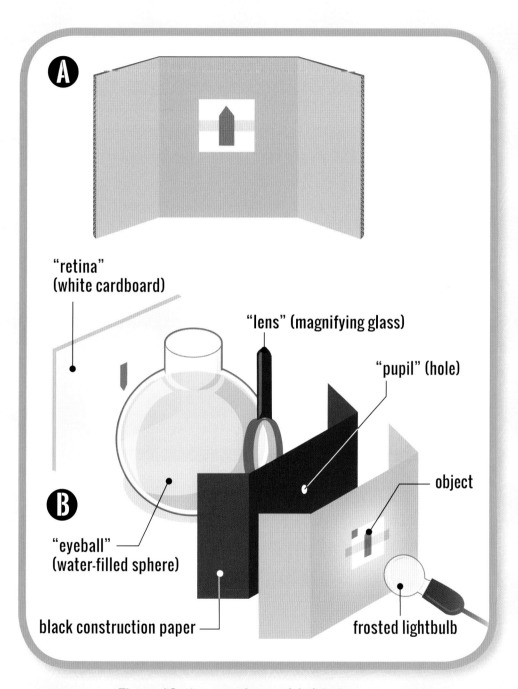

A

"retina"
(white cardboard)

"lens" (magnifying glass)

"pupil" (hole)

object

B

"eyeball"
(water-filled sphere)

black construction paper

frosted lightbulb

Figure 10. You can make a model of the human eye.

4. Place a magnifying glass representing the eye's lens between the "pupil" and the water-filled sphere. Move the sheet of white cardboard representing the eye's retina back and forth until you get a sharp image of the object. Is the object's image right side up or inverted?

In a real eye, the muscles attached to the lens make it more or less convex in order to focus images on the retina. In what other ways is this model not like a real eye?

Make a more intricate model of the human eye, with a lens that can be made more or less convex. Why is this a better model than the one you made in Experiment 3.2? Use your model to show how the human eye adjusts for viewing near and distant objects.

Make models to show how eyeglasses can correct for nearsightedness (myopia) and farsightedness (hyperopia).

3.3 Let the Light In

THINGS YOU WILL NEED:

- a partner
- well-lighted room
- flashlight
- T-pin or a large needle
- black construction paper
- well-lighted window

The black disc in the center of your iris is the pupil (Figure 9). It is the opening through which light enters your eye. The iris has muscles that can change the pupil's size (diameter). The muscles are connected to nerve cells that respond to light intensity.

1. To see how the pupils respond to light, ask a partner to sit in a chair in a well-lighted room. Ask your partner to keep his eyes open. Watch your partner's pupils as you shine a flashlight into one of his eyes. What happens to the pupils?

   Do iris muscles in the two eyes respond to light separately or together?

2. To find out, ask your partner to cover his left eye while you watch the right eye. Does the right pupil shrink when the left eye is covered? Does the left pupil shrink when the right eye is covered? Do iris muscles respond to light separately or together?

3. Here is a similar experiment you can do on yourself. Use a T-pin or a large needle to make a pinhole about 1 mm wide in a small, square piece of black construction paper 8 cm (3 in) on a side. Hold the pinhole close to the pupil of one eye. Turn your other eye toward a well-lighted window. You will see a circle of light coming through the pinhole in front of your eye.

4. Keep the pinhole in place. Close your other eye. What happens to the size of the circle of light? What happens to the size of the circle when you open the other eye?

5. How can you make the circle shrink and widen in a rhythmic manner?

6. Concentrate on the circle of light. You will see tiny clear dots with dark circles around them. The dots appear to move slowly across the circle. The dots are caused by light passing around tiny particles called floaters that are in the fluid inside the eye.

IDEAS FOR A SCIENCE FAIR PROJECT

- How are pupils involved in the red eyes sometimes seen in photographs? How can this "red eye" effect be eliminated?

- How can changes in light intensity entering one eye affect the other eye?

- Do pupils respond to stimuli other than light, such as emotions?

3.4 Binocular Vision

As you read in Chapter 2, we need two ears to locate the source of sounds. Are two eyes better than one in locating the position of an object we can see?

1. Have a partner hold a pencil so that its tip is about two feet in front of your body. Close one eye. Try to touch the pencil tip with the tip of another pencil you hold in your hand. Try the same thing with your other eye closed.

2. Keep both eyes open and again touch the end of the pencil. In which case could you more quickly and accurately touch the tip of the pencil?

3. Play catch with your partner using a Ping-Pong ball. Do you find it easier to catch the ball when you use two eyes or one? Are two eyes better than one when locating objects?

Because you have two eyes that are several centimeters apart, the images formed on the retina at the back of each eye are not quite the same. When you look at a near object, both eyes turn inward. The object's image falls on the retina in each eye as shown in Figure 11a. The nerve impulses that go to the brain from the two eyes provide a fused image. Most of the image falls on corresponding parts of each retina. The major part of the image carried to the brain is the same for both eyes. However, the right eye sees farther around the right side of the object; the left eye sees farther around the left side. Consequently, the right and left edges of the two images are different. Your brain fuses the two images and provides a three-dimensional view. It adds the parts seen only by the right and left eye to the central part to create an image that provides depth.

You can easily convince yourself that we see a slightly different world with two eyes than we do with either eye alone.

4. Use a black pen to draw a vertical line near the top of an inverted Styrofoam cup as shown in Figure 11b. To the right of that black line draw a series of vertical green lines about 0.5 cm apart. To the left of the line draw vertical red lines about 0.5 cm apart.

5. Hold the cup directly in front of your face. Hold it as close to your eyes as you can while still seeing it clearly. With both eyes open, how many green lines can you see to the right of the central black line? How many red lines can you see to the left of the black line?

6. Close your left eye. How many green lines can you see to the right of the central black line? How many red lines can you see to the left of the black line?

7. Close your right eye. How many green lines can you see to the right of the central black line? How many red lines can you see to the left of the black line?

With which eye can you see farther around the right side of the cup? With which eye can you see farther around the left side of the cup? How is what you see with two eyes different from what you see with just one eye?

A stereoscopic picture is made in a similar way. Two photographs of the same object at slightly different angles are superimposed on one another. Such a picture provides a sense of depth. Your eyes automatically provide a stereoscopic "picture." The large central part of an image falls on corresponding parts of the retinas of both eyes. Your right eye, as you have seen, sees more on its side of an object than does your left eye. Similarly, your left eye sees more on its side of an object than does your right eye. Your brain sees the central part of the image as a single image because the impulses come from corresponding cells of the retina.

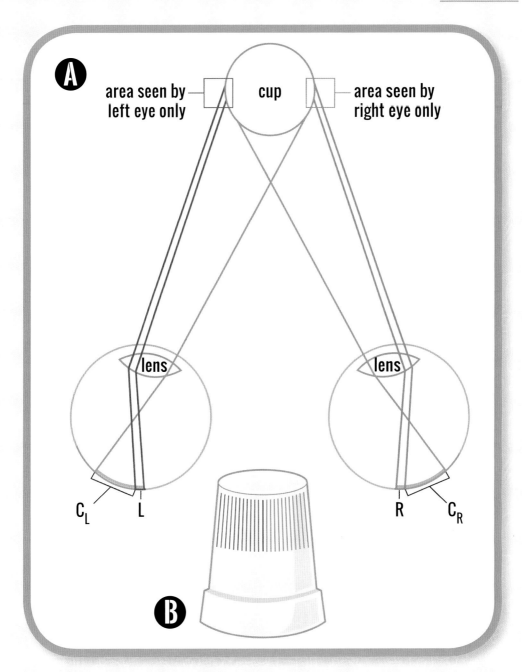

Figure 11. A) This model shows how we see depth. Regions CL and CR are parts of the image that fall on corresponding parts of both retinas. Regions L and R are parts of the image we see that fall only on the left and right retinas respectively. B) An experiment shows that the images we see in each of our eyes are slightly different.

- Find out how filmmakers can produce movies with three-dimensional effects. Why haven't such movies become popular?

- In addition to binocular vision, what other factors play a role in depth perception and estimating distances to objects?

- Make a small hole through the center of a file card with a pin. Bring this book so close to your eyes that the print appears blurred. Close one eye and hold the small hole in the card in front of your open eye. Why can you now read the print through the hole?

- Look at a distant object with both eyes. Focus on some part of the object. Now roll a sheet of paper into a tube. Hold the tube in front of one eye and again look at the same part of the distant object. Why does the tube improve your ability to see the details of a distant object?

3.5 The Eye's Blind Spot

There is a small area of your retina called the blind spot (see Figure 9). It has no cells that respond to light. It is where the fibers from the receptor cells come together and form the optic nerve that goes to the brain. What do you think you will see if an image falls on that part of your retina?

1. To find out, make a small black circle about half a centimeter in diameter on a white file card. Fill in the circle with black ink. About 8 cm (3 in) to the right of the circle, make a thick "X." The X should be about the same size as the circle.

2. Close your left eye. Hold the card at arm's length directly in front of your right eye. Fix your eye on the circle. Move the card slowly toward your right eye. You will find a point at which the X disappears. It will reappear as you move the card closer to your eye.

3. Repeat the experiment with your right eye closed. This time fix your left eye on the X, to the right of the circle. Move the card slowly toward your left eye. At some point, the circle will disappear.

Figure out a way to measure the size of the blind spot on your retina. Then measure it.

3.6 A Pair of Images

1. Roll a sheet of paper into a tight tube that has a length of 28 cm (11 in) and a diameter of about 2 cm (3/4 in).

2. Hold the tube in your right hand in front of your right eye and look out a window. Place your left hand in front of your left eye, next to the end of the tube. Your left hand will appear to have a hole in it.

3. Repeat the experiment with the tube in front of your left eye and your right hand next to the tube. Your right hand will appear to have a hole in it.

   When you do this experiment, one eye sees a window view through a hole, the other eye sees a hand. When your brain combines the two images, you see a hand with a hole in it.

4. Make a second tube identical to the first. Hold a tube in front of each eye. Look at a white wall some distance away through the tubes. You will see two white circles. Turn the tubes so the two white circles overlap. What happens to the apparent brightness of the wall? How would you explain the change in brightness?

Hold the tips of your two index fingers so they point toward one another about 30 cm (1 ft) in front of your face. Focus your eyes on a distant object. You will see what appears to be a small sausage between your fingertips. Move your fingertips just a little way apart and the sausage appears to be suspended in midair. Can you explain why?

3.7 Seeing an Afterimage

1. Sit about a meter (yard) from a glowing 60-watt frosted bulb with a white card in your hand. Stare at the bulb for about 20 seconds. Then look at the white card. You will see a brightly colored afterimage.

2. Then turn your eyes to a distant white wall. What happens to the size of the afterimage? Why do you think the size of the image changed?

3. Repeat the experiment, but this time look at the bulb with only your right eye. Close your left eye.

4. After 20 seconds, turn your head toward a white wall. Close your right eye. Look at the white wall with your left eye. Do you see an afterimage? Now close your left eye. Look at the wall with your right eye. Do you see an afterimage? Is an afterimage formed on the retina or in the brain? How do you know?

3.8 Rod Cells and Color

The central regions of our retinas are rich in cone cells that respond to color. The outer regions of the retina contain rod cells that respond to light but cannot distinguish color. According to one theory, we have three types of cone cells. There are cone cells that respond to red light, cone cells that respond to green light, and cone cells that respond to blue light.

Green light entering your eyes stimulates the cone cells sensitive to green light. If red light strikes your retina, the cone cells sensitive to red light are stimulated. And if blue light reaches your retina, the cone cells sensitive to blue light respond. The different cone cells produce nerve impulses that travel to the brain where we "see" the color.

Yellow light is a combination of red and green light. If yellow light reaches the retina, both red and green cone cells are stimulated and we see yellow.

Magenta (pinkish) light is a combination of red and blue light. If magenta light falls on our retinas, the cone cells sensitive to red and to blue light are stimulated and we see a magenta color.

Cyan (blue-green) light is a combination of green and blue light. If cyan light falls on our retinas, the cone cells sensitive to both green and blue light are stimulated and we see a cyan color. Keep this theory in mind as you do this experiment. Bear in mind, too, that sensory cells, such as cone cells, become desensitized with use.

1. Place two sheets of white paper on a table that is well lighted. On one of them, place a small, bright green square of construction paper. Stare at the green square for about 20 seconds. Then shift your gaze to the other white sheet. You will see a magenta afterimage. Why do you think the afterimage has a magenta color?

2. Repeat the experiment with a blue square. Why do you think the afterimage is yellow?

3. Repeat the experiment with a red square. Why do you think the afterimage is cyan?

4. Try to predict the color of the afterimage you will see on the white paper when you stare at a yellow square. Did you predict correctly?

5. Try to predict the color of the afterimage you will see when you stare at a cyan square. Did you predict correctly?

6. Try to predict the color of the afterimage you will see on the white paper when you stare at a magenta square. Did you predict correctly?

7. Stare at a black square. What color do you predict the afterimage will be?

8. How about a white square? What do you guess its afterimage will look like? Try it! Did you make the correct prediction?

IDEAS FOR A SCIENCE FAIR PROJECT

Design and do experiments to show that combining red and green light produces yellow; combining blue and green light produces cyan; and combining blue and red light produces magenta.

What are complementary colors for light? How can they be produced?

Red, green, and blue are the primary colors for light. Show that combining all three primaries produces white light.

What are the primary colors for pigments? What happens when the primary pigments are mixed?

3.9 Persistence of Vision

Images that form on the retina do not fade immediately. Pigments in the cone and rod cells change chemically when struck by light and give rise to nerve impulses. The chemicals formed persist for a short time, about 0.05 (1/20) second. The result is what is known as persistence of vision. It explains why the motion seen in movies, projected at a rate of 32 frames per second, seems to be continuous. You can do an experiment to see an effect caused by persistence of vision.

1. Find a mailing tube. If it has a cardboard cap, **ask an adult** to use a sharp knife to make a slit about 3 cm (2 in) long and about 3 mm (1/8 in) wide in the cap. If there is no cap, tape two pieces of black construction paper over one end. Leave a slit about 3 mm (1/8 in) wide between the two pieces.

2. Put the tube's open end close to one eye. Put one hand around that end to cushion it against your eye. The slit at the other end of the tube should be vertical. When the tube is not moving you can't see very much.

    Keep your head still as you move the tube back and forth while looking through it. Gradually increase the speed at which you swing the tube back and forth. At some speed you will find that you have a clear view of the entire scene swept out by the narrow slit.

> **THINGS YOU WILL NEED:**
> - colored object
> - set of crayons
> - dimly-lighted room

Cone cells, which are abundant in the center of the retina, respond to the colors in light. But they do not respond in dim light. Rod cells, which are found in the perimeter of the retina, respond to light, even dim light, but cannot distinguish color. You can see this for yourself.

1. Close one eye. Hold a colored object in front of your open eye. You can easily tell its color. Continue to look straight ahead as you slowly move the object along a circular path to the side of your head. You will find that you reach a point where you can see the object, but you cannot determine its color. You are seeing with rod cells.

2. Take some crayons into a room where there is very little light. You will probably be able to see the crayons, but you won't be able to identify them by color. Turn on a light so you can use your cone-cell vision. Can you now determine the color of each crayon?

Chapter 4

Digestion

It sure is a treat to share a delicious meal with your family or friends. Sharing in the shopping and cooking can be fun work, and the tastes of your favorite foods can be some of a person's fondest memories. But eating is not purely a social affair. Food nourishes the body and enables it to function.

The human body does a lot of work. Even heartbeats and breathing involve work. To do that work we need energy. That energy comes from the food we eat. It is stored in the food as chemical energy.

To make the energy in food available to the cells of our bodies, the food must first be digested. It must be changed to simpler chemicals that can pass through the cells of our stomach and intestines and into our bloodstream. The blood, as you know, circulates throughout the body. The chemicals carrying energy leave the blood and enter cells, such as muscle cells, that enable us to do work.

The digestion of food begins in the mouth and is completed in the stomach and intestines (Figure 12). How the food gets to and through our stomachs and intestines will be investigated in the next experiment.

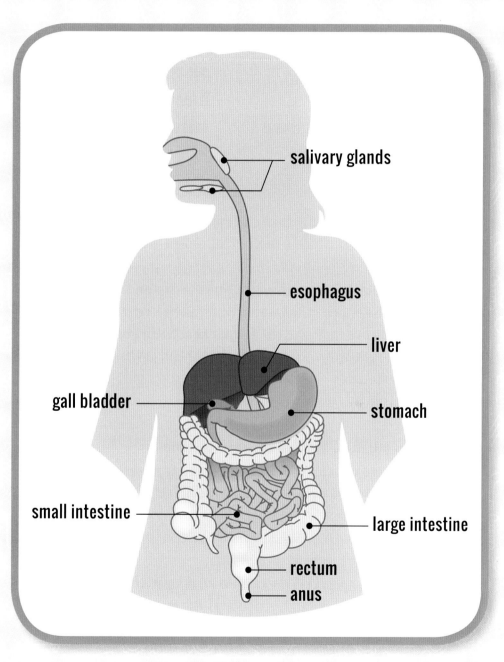

salivary glands

esophagus

liver

gall bladder

stomach

small intestine

large intestine

rectum

anus

Figure 12. The human digestive tract

4.1 Food in Your Body

THINGS YOU WILL NEED:

- plastic cup
- water
- drinking straw
- chair
- saucer
- bread
- scissors
- long, thin balloon

Is gravity needed for food to travel from your mouth to your stomach? Is it the food's weight that causes it to "fall" from mouth to stomach? Let's find out.

1. Fill a plastic cup with water. Put the cup on the floor. Put a drinking straw in the water. Bring a chair near the glass. Lie across the chair and lower your head until your mouth can reach the straw. Be sure that your head is well below the rest of your body. Try to drink the water through the straw. Were you able to drink the water?

2. Have someone hold your legs while you stand on your hands (Figure 13). Can you still drink the water?

3. Replace the cup with a saucer that has a piece of bread on it. Can you chew and swallow the bread with your head below the rest of your body? Need more evidence? Think of astronauts. They live in the space station for months at a time, a place where weights do not fall.

    If gravity isn't needed for food to reach your stomach, how does it travel through your body? The answer is peristalsis. The muscles of your esophagus, stomach, and intestines contract in a rhythmic fashion called peristalsis.

4. To see how this works, roll a piece of bread into a ball about an inch in diameter. Cut off the end of a long, thin balloon.

Figure 13. Is gravity needed for you to drink? Can you drink while standing on your hands?

Put the bread ball into the balloon. Use your fingers to squeeze the balloon together so as to move the bread along the balloon. Food moves along your digestive tract in a similar way. The muscles in the walls of your esophagus, stomach, and intestines contract and push solid and liquid foods along just as your fingers did on the bread in the balloon.

FOR A SCIENCE FAIR PROJECT

IDEA

What problems arise when someone tries to eat or drink on the space station? How do astronauts cope with these problems?

4.2 Teeth Impressions

THINGS YOU WILL NEED:

- scissors
- ruler
- Styrofoam cups
- at least one adult
- child who is about four years old
- pencil or pen
- mirror

Most babies are toothless at birth. They cannot bite off or chew food. Their diet is limited to liquids and soft foods that do not need to be chewed. Teeth enable us to enjoy a more varied diet.

1. You can make impressions of teeth. Using scissors, cut square pieces about 8 cm (3 in) on a side from Styrofoam cups. Put two pieces, one on top of the other, into your mouth. Bite down firmly on the Styrofoam pieces. Remove them from your mouth. Label the top piece "upper" and the bottom piece "lower." Compare the impressions. How can you distinguish upper teeth impressions from lower teeth impressions?

2. Collect teeth impressions from at least one adult and one child who is about four years old. How many teeth does an adult have? How many teeth does a four-year-old child have? Label the top and bottom teeth impressions and the name of the person who made them.

   As you probably remember, you lost your first set of teeth. They are gradually replaced by adult teeth beginning at five or six years of age.

3. Examine your teeth with a mirror. At the front of the jaw, find four flat teeth, known as incisors, on both upper and lower jaws. How do you think these teeth help us eat?

4. Just beyond the incisors can you find two canines on each jaw? How do canine teeth differ in appearance from incisors?

5. Farther back, look for two premolars beyond the canines on either side of both jaws. These teeth have crowns (tops) that are quite flat. They are similar to, but smaller than the four molars you can find on both jaws behind the premolars. In your late teens, four more molars, known as wisdom teeth, may appear. Some people never get their wisdom teeth, which are not needed and can be troublesome.

6. With permission, look at the teeth of a child. What teeth are missing in children that are present in adults?

    What role do teeth play in preparing food for digestion?

Some towns and cities add fluoride (a chemical) to their water. Why do they do this? What are the effects of fluoride on teeth? Does it affect other parts of the body?

4.3 **Enzymes**

A catalyst is a substance that changes the rate of a chemical reaction without being changed by the reaction. An enzyme is a biological catalyst.

1. To see the action of a catalyst, pour about 10 mL of 3-percent hydrogen peroxide (H_2O_2) into a large test tube or vial. If left by itself, hydrogen peroxide slowly decomposes into oxygen and water. That chemical reaction is shown below:

$$2H_2O_2 \rightarrow 2H_2O + O_2$$

If a catalyst is added, the reaction goes much faster. One catalyst for this reaction is manganese dioxide (MnO_2).

2. **Under adult supervision**, use a popsicle stick or something similar to add a pinch of manganese dioxide to the hydrogen peroxide. How does the manganese dioxide affect the rate of the reaction? Is the gas being generated really oxygen?

3. To find out, **under adult supervision**, repeat the experiment and then place a glowing splint into the test tube or vial. What happens? How does this test indicate that the gas is oxygen?

77

4. To see the action of an enzyme, prepare some gelatin according to the directions on the label. Before you cool the liquid, divide it in half. Put a piece of kiwi fruit in one of the two halves. Place both liquids in the refrigerator overnight. The next day, look at the two gelatin samples. Look carefully at the area around the kiwi fruit. What evidence do you have that kiwi fruit contains an enzyme that breaks down gelatin?

In the next experiment, you will look for the action of an enzyme found in saliva.

4.4 Digestive Enzymes

THINGS YOU WILL NEED:

- **an adult**
- safety goggles
- plastic gloves
- saltine cracker
- 3 small glasses or jars with wide mouths
- spoon
- tablespoon
- warm water
- tincture of iodine (obtain from a pharmacy)
- notebook
- pen or pencil

You will use iodine in this experiment. Iodine is poisonous and stains flesh. You should wear safety goggles and plastic gloves while doing this experiment. **Do not do this experiment without an adult.**

The three basic types of food we eat are carbohydrates, fats, and proteins. Carbohydrates consist of starches and sugars. Amylase, an enzyme found in saliva and in the intestines, changes starch to complex sugars (disaccharides). The complex sugars are changed to simple sugars (monosaccharides) by other enzymes in the intestines. The simple sugars can pass through the intestinal walls and enter the bloodstream. Enzymes also change fats and proteins into simpler substances that can enter the bloodstream.

In this experiment, you will use the amylase in your saliva to see if you can detect its effect on starch. Starch is a common component of bread, crackers, potatoes, and pasta.

1. Break a saltine cracker in half. Break one half into small pieces and drop them into a small glass or jar with a wide mouth. Use a spoon to crush the cracker into tiny bits. Add a tablespoonful of warm water to the crushed cracker and stir.

2. Put on safety goggles and plastic gloves. **Under adult supervision**, add three drops of tincture of iodine and stir. **Iodine is poisonous. Do not let iodine touch your mouth.** If the cracker contains starch, you will see the iodine turn to a very dark blue color. Iodine is used to test for starch.

3. Mix the other half of the cracker with your saliva by chewing it for at least one minute. It should become a wet, mushy mass. Spit half of the mushy cracker into a second glass or jar. Spit the other half into a third glass or jar.

4. To each of these two glasses or jars add one tablespoonful of warm water and stir. To one glass or jar add three drops of tincture of iodine and stir. Compare the color you see here with the color you saw when you added iodine to the unchewed cracker.

5. Leave the other diluted mushy mass for one hour. Then add three drops of tincture of iodine and stir. How does the color you see here compare with the color you saw when you added iodine to the other two samples you tested?

4.5 **Food for Energy**

In this experiment you can see that food really does contain energy.

1. To find the energy stored in a corn puff, build a calorimeter like the one shown in Figure 14. A small, empty (6-oz) frozen juice can with a metal bottom and cardboard sides can be used to hold cold water. **Ask an adult** to use a nail to make holes through opposite sides of the can near its open top. Push a pencil through the holes. The pencil will support this small can inside a large empty can.

2. **Ask an adult** to remove both ends of the large can.

3. Use a can opener to make four or five triangular holes along the bottom sides of the large can as shown. The holes

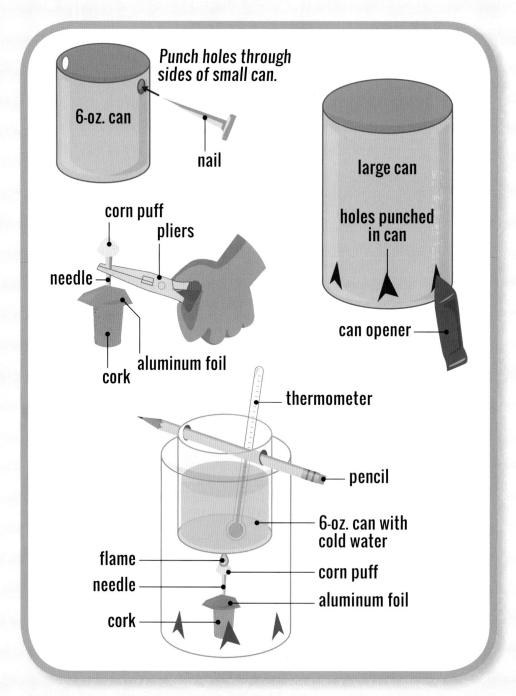

Punch holes through sides of small can.

6-oz. can

nail

corn puff

pliers

needle

cork

aluminum foil

large can

holes punched in can

can opener

thermometer

pencil

6-oz. can with cold water

flame

needle

cork

corn puff

aluminum foil

Figure 14. To find the energy stored in food, burn the food and capture the heat released in a known mass of water.

allow air to enter the can. The bright interior of the large can will reflect some of the heat that might otherwise escape to the surrounding air.

4. Cover the small end of a cork with a piece of aluminum foil. Using pliers, force the eye of a large sewing needle through the foil and into the cork as shown.

5. Next, break a corn puff in half. Weigh one of the halves on a sensitive balance. If the balance is not sensitive enough to weigh one corn puff, weigh a hundred of them and divide by 200 to find the weight of half of one.

6. Gently push the half corn puff onto the sharp upright end of the needle.

7. Pour 150 grams (g) of cold water into the small can. Since 1.0 mL of water weighs 1 g, you can simply measure out a volume of 150 mL (3.5 oz) of cold water and pour it into the can.

8. Place a laboratory thermometer in the can and measure and record the water's temperature.

9. **Ask an adult** to light the corn puff with a match. Immediately place the large can over the burning corn puff. Quickly put the small can with the water into the large can as shown in Figure 14. Stir the water gently with the thermometer until after the corn puff goes out. Record the final temperature of the water.

10. Does any of the corn puff remain? If it does, weigh it or estimate its mass to find how much of the corn puff did not burn.

The mass of the water and its temperature change can be used to calculate the heat released by the burning corn puff. Remember, a calorie is the amount of heat needed to raise the temperature of 1 g of water by 1°C. If the temperature of the 150 g of water increased by 10°C, then the corn puff provided 1,500 calories (150 g x 10°C) of energy. How much heat energy did the burning corn puff release?

What mass of corn puff, in grams, provided the heat absorbed by the water? How much heat was produced per gram of corn puff burned? Is the value of the heat per gram obtained from your data higher or lower than the actual value? What makes you think so?

Nutritionists measure energy in what are called large calories or Calories. A Calorie with a capital "C" is the heat needed to raise the temperature of 1 kilogram of water by 1°C. It is 1,000 times bigger than a calorie with a small "c." How many Calories are provided by 1 gram of corn puff according to your data?

Under adult supervision, find the heat released, in calories per gram, by a peanut, a walnut, and a cashew. How do they compare with the energy per gram from a corn puff?

With an adult present, use the equipment in Experiment 4.5 to measure the amount of heat released per gram of candle wax for several different kinds of candles. If we can obtain energy from candle wax, why don't we use it as a food?

4.6 Liquid Waste

As food passes through our intestines, much of it is absorbed into our bloodstream and carried to the cells of our body. The solid waste that remains is excreted as feces through the anus at the very end of the large intestine. Carbon dioxide, which forms when food is oxidized to obtain energy, is excreted through our lungs. Water, like carbon dioxide, is formed when food is oxidized. Some water is excreted as sweat and in vapor we exhale from our lungs. Some is mixed with solids in feces. But water is also used to dissolve other wastes that are excreted by the action of our kidneys.

Your kidneys—a pair of reddish-brown organs that lie against the back of your abdomen—filter your blood. The filtering removes waste materials such as excess minerals, nitrogen-containing wastes (ammonia, urea, uric acid), and water. The kidneys retain vital elements and compounds essential to your health. Urine is the liquid waste produced by the kidneys. It flows from the kidneys along tubes (ureters) to the bladder where it is stored (Figure 15). As urine accumulates, the bladder walls stretch, stimulating nerves leading to your brain that indicate the need to urinate. When you urinate, the bladder contracts forcing urine out of your body through a tube (the urethra).

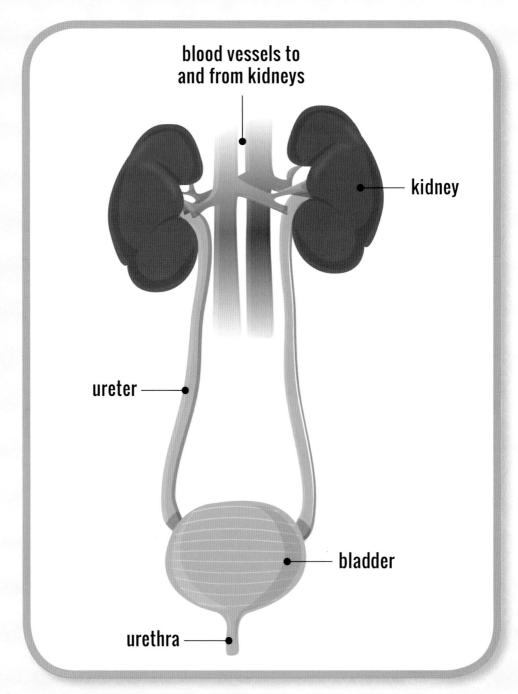

blood vessels to
and from kidneys

kidney

ureter

bladder

urethra

Figure 15. Kidneys filter blood and produce urine, which travels to the bladder through the ureters.

Urine is 95 percent water. Although bacteria sometimes contaminate urine, the liquid is normally sterile. You can examine and test your urine to see what it says about your state of health.

1. Normally urine is a clear, light-yellow liquid. Examine a sample of your urine in a clear container. Urine excreted in the morning after a long night's rest may have a deeper color than samples collected during the day. Can you explain why?

   Urine that is cloudy, reddish, greenish-yellow, or golden brown in color may indicate disorders that should be checked by a doctor.

2. If possible, obtain from a pharmacy, your school science department, or a science supply house (see Appendix), pH paper (range 5–9) and various urinary test strips. The pH paper will allow you to test the acidity of your urine. The various urinary test strips will enable you to test for glucose sugar (common in people with diabetes), protein, ketones, white blood cells, bilirubin, and other factors. What do positive results for any of these tests indicate?

Design an experiment to find out if weather, particularly temperature, affects the amount of urine you excrete.

Design an experiment to show that water is excreted through your lungs as well as in urine.

Chapter 5

Keep Experimenting with the Human Body

So far, you have experimented with a few different parts of the human body. You have seen that circulation and respiration are key systems in the body that deal with the heart and the lungs. Your senses, especially your eyes, involve magnificent orchestrations between organs of your body. Food nourishes the body, and you have looked at the science involved with getting energy from the things you eat. What else is there to study?

This chapter contains more experiments involving the human body. They come in a variety of topics. You will investigate reflexes, measure your reaction speed, investigate muscle pairs, experience a strange sensation, and find where your body's mass is centered.

In the first experiment, you will investigate how two hands and a moving target may be better than one hand and a stationary target. Let's get started.

5.1 **Hit the Target**

You might think that hitting a stationary target is easier than hitting a moving one. But that is not always true.

1. Stick a sewing needle into a piece of cardboard or some other surface that will hold it steady. Using your dominant hand (your right hand, if you are right-handed), thread the needle using a short length of thread. Keep your other hand behind your back.

2. Remove the needle from the cardboard and the thread from the needle.

3. Use both hands to thread the needle.

Was threading the needle easier with a fixed needle or with one you could move with your non-dominant hand? Why do you think it was easier?

5.2 The Diving Reflex

> ### THINGS YOU WILL NEED:
>
> - dish pan at least 25 cm (10 in) wide and 8 cm (3 in) deep
> - cold water
> - ice cubes
> - towel
> - kitchen counter
> - clock or watch with second hand
> - a partner
> - notebook
> - pen or pencil

In Experiment 3.3, you saw how the pupil responds to light and dark. This response is a reflex. It is involuntary and not something you are aware of.

There is a reflex you are more aware of. When your doctor strikes a point just below your knee with a rubber hammer, your leg straightens.

There is also a reflex, known as the diving reflex, that has saved a number of people from drowning. Victims who have been under cold water for 40 minutes have been revived. You can experience this reflex without diving. **Do not do this experiment if you have a heart condition.**

1. Find a dishpan at least 25 cm (10 in) wide and 8 cm (3 in) deep. Fill it with cold water and cover the water with ice cubes. Place the pan on a towel on a kitchen counter. After five minutes of resting, have a partner take your pulse for 15 seconds and record your heart rate.

2. Take a deep breath and hold it. Put your face into the ice water. Be sure your nose and eyes are under the cold water.

3. After 30 seconds, have your partner tap your back. Remove your face from the cold water. Have your partner

immediately take your pulse and record your heart rate. What happened to your heart rate after your face was in cold water?

Based on this experiment, what is the diving reflex and how does it work? How do you think this reflex has saved the lives of people who fell through the ice on frozen ponds?

5.3 **Fast Reaction**

> ## THINGS YOU WILL NEED:
> - desk or table
> - a partner
> - 30-cm (12-in) ruler
> - notebook
> - pen or pencil

How fast can you react to a stimulus? You can find out by doing this experiment.

1. Rest the side of your hand on the edge of a desk or table as shown in Figure 16. Your thumb and fingers should be about an inch apart. Your partner will hold a 30-cm (12-in) ruler, which he will drop. The zero end of the ruler should be even with your thumb and index finger.

2. Watch the lower end of the ruler. When your partner releases the ruler, you will see the ruler begin to fall. As soon as you see it start to fall, bring your thumb and fingers together.

3. How far did the ruler fall before you caught it? You can tell how far it fell by seeing what centimeter or inch line on the ruler lies under your thumb or index finger. The faster you react, the shorter the distance the ruler will fall.

4. Record the distance the ruler fell. Then repeat the experiment four more times. For each trial, record the distance the ruler fell. Then calculate the average distance the ruler fell. Use Table 1 to determine your average reaction time.

   Suppose you catch the ruler at 11 in. How can you estimate your reaction time?

5. One way is to use Table 1 to plot a graph of distance versus reaction time. Join the points with a smooth curve. The graph will then give you the reaction time for any distance the ruler fell before being caught.

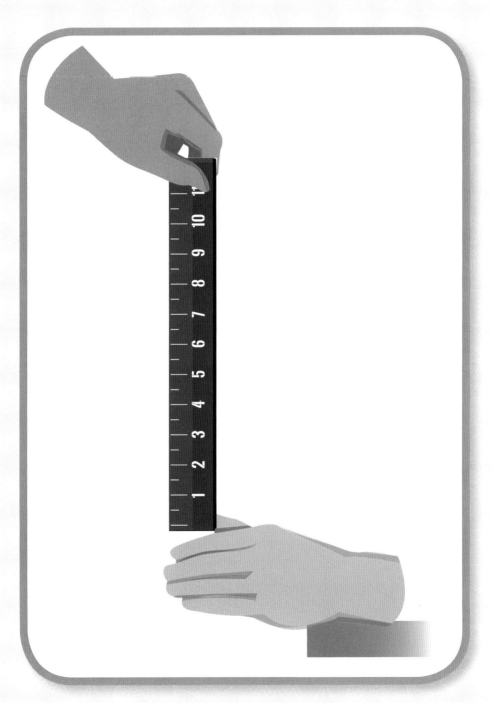

Figure 16. Measure your reaction speed.

TABLE 1.

Reaction times for various distances a ruler falls before being caught.

Distance ruler fell (inches)	Distance ruler fell (centimeters)	Reaction time (seconds)
2	5.0	0.102
4	10.0	0.144
6	15.0	0.177
8	20.0	0.204
10	25.0	0.228
12	30.0	0.250

Based on the data you collected, what is your reaction time?

6. Repeat the experiment using your other hand. Does your dominant hand react faster than your other hand?

7. Repeat the experiment to test your partner's reaction time. How does it compare with yours?

8. Try the experiment with a number of different people. Choose people of different gender and age. Measure their reaction times for each of their hands. Does hand dominance affect reaction time? Does age affect reaction time? Do girls react faster than boys? What other factors might affect reaction time?

9. Your reaction time is related to the time for a visual nerve signal to move to your brain from your eye and for another nerve signal to travel from your brain to the muscles in your forearm. Using a tape measure and the data you have collected, make an estimate of the speed at which nerve impulses travel along nerve fibers.

IDEAS FOR A SCIENCE FAIR PROJECT

- Measure your reaction time at different times of the day, such as just after you get up, just before lunch, late afternoon, and just before going to bed. Does time of day affect your reaction time? If it does, can you explain why?

- Explain how the reaction times for different distances of fall in Table 1 were determined.

- Do people who play video games have shorter reaction times than others?

5.4 **Voluntary Muscles**

Many of the muscles involved in reflexes are involuntary, but movements that we make consciously are with voluntary muscles. For example, we bend our joints (places where bones connect) using muscles. To bend or straighten your arm or leg, to turn your head left or right, up or down, you need pairs of muscles. One muscle contracts and bends your arm, another muscle contracts and straightens your arm.

1. You can feel the muscle that bends your arm. With your left arm straight, place the palm of your right hand on the upper part of your left arm above the inside of your elbow. To bend your left arm, the biceps muscle on the upper part of that arm must contract. Your right hand can feel your left biceps muscle contract and "make a muscle."

2. Repeat the experiment with your fingers on the inside of your elbow. You can feel the tendon that connects your biceps to the bones of your lower arm. The biceps pulls on the tendon, which, in turn, pulls on the lower arm bones.

3. Put your right hand on the back of your bent left arm. Straighten your left arm slowly. Feel the triceps muscle on the back of the arm. Its contraction causes the arm to straighten.

Muscles come in pairs, but one member of the pair is often stronger than the other. Use a bathroom scale to measure muscle strength. For example, measure the force you can create with the muscles that push your foot forward. Compare it with the force used to push your foot backwards. Compare the strength of your biceps and triceps. Other pairs you might compare are those that turn your toes up or down, open or close your hands, straighten or bend your leg, and so on.

5.5 **A Pencil Trick**

THINGS YOU WILL NEED:
- pencil
- a partner

1. Find a pencil. Close your eyes. Hold a pencil between the tips of your thumb and all four fingers. You know there is a single pencil even though you feel it with five separate fingertips. Your brain somehow builds a complete "image" of the pencil even though it receives touch sensations from five independent sources. Your brain puts all the impulses together and perceives what it expects it should be feeling.

2. Now try this. Ask a partner to cross the index and middle fingers of one hand as shown in Figure 17 and then close his eyes. Hold a pencil between the tips of your partner's crossed fingers.

3. Ask him how many pencils he feels. He will probably say, "Two." Ask him to open his eyes. He will be surprised to find that there is only one pencil.

4. Let your partner do the same experiment on you. Even though you know that there is only one pencil, you will feel two when your eyes are closed. How would you explain the results of this experiment?

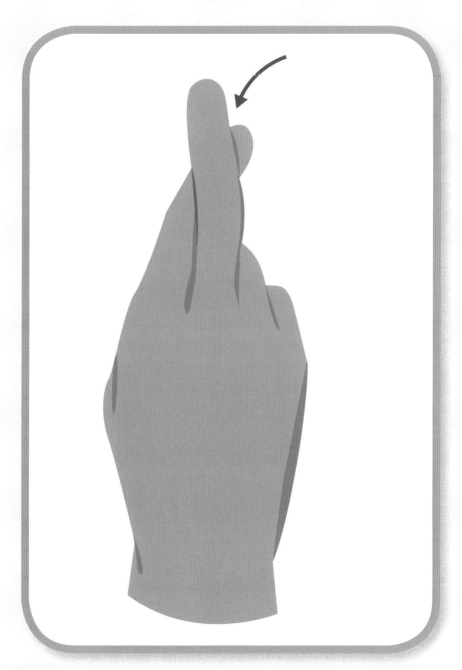

Figure 17. Cross the middle and index fingers. To feel something weird, place a pencil between them.

5.6 Center of Mass

Every object has a center of mass (COM)—a point where all its mass can be considered to be concentrated. It is the point in an object where it can balance and have no tendency to rotate one way or the other. It is also the point where you can pick up the object without it turning in any way. The COM of a sphere, such as Earth or a baseball, is its center. Where do you think the COM of a 30-cm (12-in) ruler is located?

1. To confirm your guess, place what you think is the ruler's COM on your outstretched finger. Is the ruler balanced? If it is, you have correctly predicted its COM.

2. Not all objects are as uniform as a sphere or a ruler. Use shears to cut a sheet of cardboard into an irregular shape such as the one shown in Figure 18.

3. To find the COM of such an irregular shape, make a plumb line using a pin, thread, and a heavy washer (see Figure 18). Tie one end of the thread to the pin, the other end to the washer. Use the pin to hang the irregular shape on something such as a bulletin board. The shape should be able to swing freely. Use a pencil to mark the thread's path

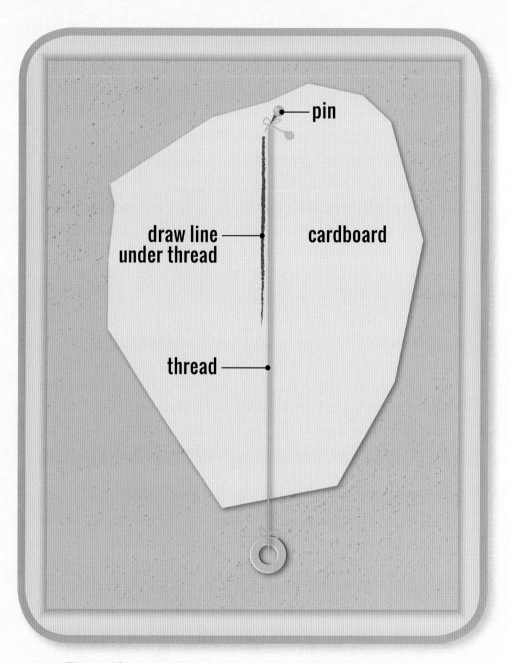

Figure 18. You can find the center of mass of an object that has an irregular shape.

along the cardboard. The washer at the end of the plumb line is attracted by gravity toward Earth's center so the line you drew will have that direction.

4. Next, hang the shape from a number of different points after turning it a few degrees. Mark the thread-line for each position. You will find that the lines all meet (or nearly meet) at one point. This point, which was always under the pin supporting the irregular shape, is its COM.

5. To be certain this method works, take down the cardboard. Put the point where the lines meet on your fingertip. Does the shape balance on your finger? If it does, what does that tell you about the point on the cardboard? Can you balance the cardboard at any other point?

6. The human body has a center of mass. To find your body's COM, put a pillow on the back of a chair. **Ask an adult** to hold the chair in place. Then lie with your lower abdomen on the pillow with your arms at your side. Your COM is likely a few centimeters below your belly button. Adjust your position until your body is balanced on the back of the chair. When your body is balanced on the chair, you know your COM lies directly above the back of the chair. Of course, that point is inside your body about halfway from your abdomen to your back.

   Normally, you keep your COM above and between your two feet. By doing so, there is no tendency for your body to rotate (fall).

   How does your body respond when your COM is beyond points of support?

7. Stand in front of a full-length mirror. Lift one foot so you have only one point of support. How does your body respond?

More Human Body COM Experiments to Try

8. Stand with your heels against a wall. Try to bend over and touch your toes. What happens?

9. To see why it happens, watch someone else (or yourself in a full-length mirror) as she bends to touch her toes. What happens to her COM as she lowers her shoulders and arms toward her toes? What happens to the position of her COM as she bends over? Why must her COM move if she is to remain on her feet?

10. Watch the same person move as she goes from a normal flat-footed stance to one where she is standing on her toes. How does her body move? Why does it move that way?

11. Try to predict what will happen if you stand with your toes against a wall and then try to stand on your toes. Try it! Was your prediction correct?

12. A fun thing to try at a party or in science class can help locate a person's COM. Ask someone to get on the floor on his hands and knees. Place a deck of cards or a blackboard eraser on its end one cubit in front of his knees. (A cubit is the distance from a person's elbow to the fingertips of his outstretched hand.) The person, with both hands behind his back, is to try to tip the cards or eraser over with his nose. Keep your eyes on the participant's COM as he attempts to knock over the cards or eraser. How is his COM related to his ability to maintain his balance? Try it with a few other people.

    How many people can do this? What does it have to do with a person's COM? Do women and girls seem to be able to do this more easily than men and boys? Does COM seem to be gender related?

Answers to Questions

Experiment 1.1

Your heart pumps 130 mL/beat x 70 beats/min = 9,100 milliliters per minute.

9,100 mL/min ÷ 1,000 mL/L = 9.1 liters per minute
9.1 L/min × 1.06 qt/L = 9.6 quarts per minute.
9.6 qt/min ÷ 4 qt/gal = 2.4 gallons per minute
9.1 L/min × 60 min/h = 546 liters per hour.
546 L/h × 24 h/day = 13,100 liters per day.

Experiment 1.4

When you pull down on the "diaphragm," the chest cavity expands in volume. This makes the air pressure inside the chest cavity less than the air pressure outside. As a result, outside air moves into the "lung." When the diaphragm moves up, the chest cavity shrinks and the pressure in the lung becomes greater than the air pressure outside and air flows out of the lung.

Science Supply Companies

Arbor Scientific
PO Box 2750
Ann Arbor, MI 48106-2750
(800) 367-6695
arborsci.com

Carolina Biological Supply Co.
PO Box 6010
Burlington, NC 27215-3398
(800) 334-5551
carolina.com

Connecticut Valley Biological
   Supply Co., Inc.
82 Valley Road
PO Box 326
Southampton, MA 01073
(800) 628-7748
ctvalleybio.com

Educational Innovations, Inc.
5 Francis J. Clarke Circle
Bethel, CT 06801
(203) 748-3224
teachersource.com

Fisher Science Education
300 Industry Drive
Pittsburgh, PA 15275
(800) 955-1177
fishersci.com

Frey Scientific
80 Northwest Blvd.
Nashua, NH 03061-3000
(800) 225-3739
freyscientific.com

Nasco
901 Janesville Ave.
Fort Atkinson, WI 53538
(800) 558-9595
enasco.com/science

Scientifics Direct
532 Main Street
Tonawanda, NY 14150
(800) 818-4955
scientificsonline.com

Ward's Science
5100 West Henrietta Road
PO Box 92912
Rochester, NY 14692-9012
(800) 962-2660
wardsci.com

aorta The body's largest artery. It carries blood rich in oxygen from the heart's left ventricle to all other arteries except the pulmonary artery.

arteries Blood vessels that carry blood from the heart to various parts of the body.

atria (singular: *atrium*) The two (right and left) thin-walled upper chambers of the heart that pump blood into the ventricles.

auditory nerve A nerve that carries signals created by sound from the inner ear to the brain.

blind spot A small area of your retina that has no cells that respond to light.

blood pressure The pressure of blood in arteries. Systolic pressure occurs when the heart contracts, forcing blood in to the arteries. It is greater than diastolic pressure, which occurs just before the heart contracts, when the pressure in the arteries is at a minimum.

breathing rate The number of breaths taken per minute.

catalyst A substance that changes the rate of a chemical reaction without being changed by the reaction. An enzyme is a biological catalyst.

center of mass A point where all an object's mass can be considered to be located. It is the point where an object is balanced and has no tendency to rotate.

choroid coat A layer of tissue inside the eye's sclerotic coat. It contains blood vessels and dark pigment that reduces the reflection of light entering the eye.

ciliary muscles The muscles that control the shape of the eye's lens.

cone cells Cells in the central regions of the retina that respond to colored light and cause impulses to travel to the brain.

cornea The front part of the sclerotic coat, which is clear and allows light to enter. It also bends (refracts) light.

diaphragm The sheet-like muscle that separates the chest and abdomen.

fovea The center of the retina, which has an abundance of cone cells. It is the region where our best vision is located.

iris The colored part of the eye that surrounds the pupil.

kidneys A pair of reddish-brown organs that filter your blood and remove waste materials while retaining vital elements and compounds.

lens A part of the eye that refracts light, causing images to form on the retina.

mitral valve The valve between the atrium and ventricle on the right side of the heart.

optic nerve The nerve that carries impulses from the eye's retina to the brain.

peristalsis The rhythmic contraction of the muscles of your esophagus, stomach, and intestines.

pulmonary artery The artery that carries blood from the heart's right ventricle to the lungs.

pulmonary veins The veins that carry blood from the lungs to the heart's left atrium.

pulse rate The number of times the heart beats each minute.

pupil An opening in the iris that allows light to reach the lens of the eye.

resonance   The vibrational response of any object to its natural frequency of vibration.

retina   The innermost layer of the eye. It contains rod and cone cells that respond to light and send nerve impulses to the brain.

rod cells   Cells in the outer regions of the retina that respond to light but do not distinguish among colors of different wavelength.

sclerotic coat   The white, rigid, outside layer of the eye. It gives the eye its spherical shape.

semicircular canals   Three canals at right angles to one another that contain fluid. Movement causes the fluids to push against tiny hairlike sensors that send nerve impulses to the part of the brain that controls muscles that help you maintain balance.

sphygmomanometer   A device used to measure blood pressure.

tricuspid valve   The valve between the heart's right atrium and ventricle.

ureters   Tubes that carry urine from the kidneys to the bladder, where it is stored.

urethra   A tube that carries urine from the bladder to outside the body.

urine   The liquid waste produced by the kidneys. It flows from the kidneys along tubes called ureters.

veins   Blood vessels that carry blood to the heart from various parts of the body.

vena cava   The large veins (superior and inferior) that carry blood to the heart's right atrium.

ventricles   The two thick-walled (right and left) chambers of the heart that pump blood into the aorta and pulmonary artery.

Further Reading

Books

Barnes-Svarney, Patricia L. *The Handy Anatomy Answer Book*. Detroit, MI: Visible Ink Press, 2016.

Buczynski, Sandy. *Designing a Winning Science Fair Project*. Ann Arbor, MI: Cherry Lake Publishing, 2014.

Butterfield, Moira. *Amazing Body*. New York, NY: Little Bee Books, 2015.

Meister, Cari. *Totally Wacky Facts About the Human Body*. North Mankato, MN: Capstone, 2016.

Rocket, Paul. *100 Trillion Good Bacteria Living on the Human Body*. Chicago, IL: Capstone Raintree, 2016.

Websites

BBC Future—Human Body
bbc.com/future/tags/humanbody
Learn even more about the amazing humany body.

Brain Pop
brainpop.com/science/scientificinquiry/scientificmethod
Have fun learning about the scientific method.

The Exploratorium
exploratorium.edu/snacks/subject/biology
A great set of links to more biology activities and facts.

Index